BLUE BANNER
BIOGRAPHY

Stephenie
MEYER

Tamra Orr

Mitchell Lane
PUBLISHERS
P.O. Box 196
Hockessin, Delaware 19707
Visit us on the web: www.mitchelllane.com
Comments? email us: mitchelllane@mitchelllane.com

Mitchell Lane
PUBLISHERS

Printing   1   2   3   4   5   6   7   8   9

Blue Banner Biographies

Akon
Alicia Keys
Allen Iverson
Ashanti
Ashlee Simpson
Ashton Kutcher
Avril Lavigne
Beyoncé
Blake Lively
Bow Wow
Brett Favre
Britney Spears
Carrie Underwood
Chris Brown
Chris Daughtry
Christina Aguilera
Christopher Paul Curtis
Ciara
Clay Aiken
Cole Hamels
Condoleezza Rice
Corbin Bleu
Daniel Radcliffe
David Ortiz
David Wright
Derek Jeter
Drew Brees
Eminem
Eve

Fergie
Flo Rida
Gwen Stefani
Ice Cube
Ja Rule
Jamie Foxx
Jay-Z
Jennifer Lopez
Jessica Simpson
J. K. Rowling
Joe Flacco
John Legend
Johnny Depp
Justin Berfield
Justin Timberlake
Kanye West
Kate Hudson
Keith Urban
Kelly Clarkson
Kenny Chesney
Kristen Stewart
Lady Gaga
Lance Armstrong
Leona Lewis
Lil Wayne
Lindsay Lohan
Mariah Carey
Mario
Mary J. Blige

Mary-Kate and Ashley Olsen
Megan Fox
Miguel Tejada
Missy Elliott
Nancy Pelosi
Natasha Bedingfield
Orianthi
Orlando Bloom
P. Diddy
Peyton Manning
Pink
Queen Latifah
Rihanna
Robert Pattinson
Ron Howard
Sean Kingston
Selena
Shakira
Shia LaBeouf
Shontelle Layne
Soulja Boy Tell 'Em
Stephenie Meyer
Taylor Swift
T.I.
Timbaland
Tim McGraw
Toby Keith
Usher
Vanessa Anne Hudgens
Zac Efron

Library of Congress Cataloging-in-Publication Data
Orr, Tamra.
  Stephenie Meyer / by Tamra Orr.
    p. cm. — (Blue Banner biographies)
  Includes bibliographical references and index.
  ISBN 978-1-58415-907-0 (library bound)
  1. Meyer, Stephenie, 1973– —Juvenile literature. 2. Authors, American—21st century—Biography—Juvenile literature. 3. Young adult fiction—Authorship—Juvenile literature. 4. Meyer, Stephenie, 1973–5. Authors, American—21st century. 6. Young adult fiction—Authorship. I. Title.
  PS3613.E979Z83 2010
  813'.6—dc22
  [B]
                                                                                              2010014896

ABOUT THE AUTHOR: Tamra Orr is the author of almost 200 nonfiction books for readers of all ages, including more than two dozen for Mitchell Lane Publishers. Several of her titles have won awards. Orr has a degree in English and Secondary Education from Ball State University in Muncie, Indiana. She lives in the Pacific Northwest with her four kids, husband, dog, and cat. When she isn't researching and writing a book, she is usually reading one or walking outside to gaze at the beautiful snow-covered mountains.

PUBLISHER'S NOTE: The following story has been thoroughly researched, and to the best of our knowledge represents a true story. While every possible effort has been made to ensure accuracy, the publisher will not assume liability for damages caused by inaccuracies in the data and makes no warranty on the accuracy of the information contained herein. This story has not been authorized or endorsed by Stephenie Meyer.

Blue Banner Biography

A haunting dream roused Stephenie Meyer from her weary existence to a more exciting life.

An Amazing Dream

Storybooks and Disney movies are full of tales of the "rags to riches" girl—the one who one day is sweeping floors and fireplaces and the next is living in a castle with Prince Charming and wearing a crown. That kind of story does not come true very often in real life, but in the case of Stephenie Meyer, it did.

It was not an easy period in Meyer's life. The previous few months had been tough—due to several small children to raise, a husband who was sick, and a fall that had broken her arm. "It wasn't a great time . . . ," she recalled in 2007 to Megan Irwin from the *Phoenix New Times.* "I'd put on so much weight with the two babies. My thirtieth birthday was coming up and I was so not ready to face being thirty. I didn't feel I had much going for me. I had my kids, but there wasn't much I was doing."

Although Meyer enjoyed being a wife to Christiaan, or Pancho, as he is known, as well as mother to three boys, Gabe and Seth (with son Eli on the way), she felt like something was still missing in her life. She felt she was meant to be doing something else, but she was not sure what it was. She had tried painting in the past, and although she was okay at it, it did not feel right. She had even joined a scrapbooking group to see if that was a hobby she could enjoy. It wasn't — and she was frustrated.

On June 1, 2003, everything changed.

After a long day, a weary Meyer crawled into bed. That night, her life changed in ways she could never have imagined. "It feels kind of funny, but I had this dream," she recalled years later on her online website. "I even remember which day it was, because I had swim lessons starting that day and all kinds of other stuff going on. It was early in the morning. I woke up and it was just so *vivid*. . . . Though I had a million things to do, I stayed in bed, thinking about the dream. Unwillingly, I eventually got up and did the immediate necessities, and then put everything that I possibly could on the back burner and sat down at the computer to write — something I hadn't done in so long that I wondered why I was bothering."

The first line that Meyer wrote when she sat down in front of the computer was, "In the sunlight, he was shocking." Fans all over the world will recognize that as the first line of Chapter 13 in Meyer's first book in the Twilight series. As Meyer explained to Rick Margolis at *School Library Journal*, "It's the scene in the meadow. So I really got the whole character of Edward just entirely laid out for me. He was there. Bella took a little bit more development. I just kind of sat down and wrote the book from that scene through to the end, and then I went back and wrote the beginning to make sense of it."

"It was odd because it was so coherent, it was a really complicated conversation, and because I don't ever dream about vampires," she continues on her website. "I woke up and I was just wrapped up with the idea of what was going to happen next. Was he going to kill her or were they going to be together? . . . when I found writing, it was like I had just

Meyer had no idea that a simple dream would be the key to finding everything else she wanted in life. Writing was the missing piece she had been searching for.

found my favorite flavor of ice cream. All of a sudden, there it is: '*This* is what I should have been doing for the last thirty years. What was I thinking?' So I just kept going with it."

There was no way for Meyer to know that when she woke from that dream and wrote the first line, she was making as dramatic a step as when Cinderella slipped on her glass slipper or Belle stepped into the Beast's castle. Her life was about to change completely.

Before the glitz and glamour, Meyer grew up in a humble American household. Through Edward, she would find immortality—of the literary kind.

Being a Bookworm

Stephenie Morgan was born the day before Christmas 1973 in Hartford, Connecticut. She is the second oldest, with five brothers and sisters. In a biography about the author, she describes her family as like television's *Brady Bunch* because there were three boys and three girls. The only thing that they didn't have was a maid named Alice!

Parents Stephen and Candy Morgan took their growing family and moved across the country from Connecticut to Arizona when Stephenie was four years old. Stephen, a financial planner, was offered a better-paying position in the hot, desert state. The Morgans believed that all of their children should learn to do family chores from an early age. As the second to oldest, Stephenie often found herself in the position of baby-sitter, but she did not mind looking after her four younger siblings. It gave her a lot of practice for one day becoming a mother. "It was a really nice childhood," she recalled in an interview with *CBS Sunday Morning*. "My parents were good parents."

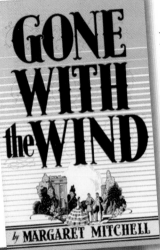

Devout members of the Church of Latter Day Saints, the family attended many church events and were active in the Mormon community. The Morgans had some strict rules in place, such as not allowing their children to listen to music that they had not approved. Stephenie did not mind all the rules, however. She far preferred to spend time reading than anything else. She tended to spend almost every spare moment reading, sometimes tearing through as many as four books a week—none of them particularly short, either. "I always had a feeling that reading was an exciting thing, and I loved big, fat books," she recalled in an interview with Tony-Allen Mills of *Times Online*. "I went from *Gone with the Wind* to *Little Women* to *Pride and Prejudice* because they were the biggest books my parents had and they were stories that were not going to end so fast."

Perhaps her love for long, never-ending stories is the reason her own books usually run to 400 pages or more. "My father used to read us some stories at night," she revealed in an interview with Benjamin Locoge from the magazine *Paris Match*. "He always stopped reading when the suspense would get real high. But I was so anxious to see what happened next that I would sneak down, get the book, and read ahead."

Her father remembers his daughter's passion for books. "She was kind of in her own little world," he stated in an interview with *The Arizona Republic*'s Jaimee Rose. "If she was in a good book, she was perfectly happy off by herself, enmeshing herself in that world."

"Reading was my only training in fiction writing. I never took a class or read a book on how to write," Meyer admitted to Deb Smouse at *All Things Girl.* "I just absorbed the basics from reading thousands of other people's stories."

Meyer attended Chaparral High School from 1989 to 1992. Although not a lot has been reported about her high school days, she had made occasional comments in magazine, television, and newspaper interviews that she often felt like her character of Bella—a somewhat clumsy outsider. She describes it as the kind of place where, at the start of each school year, students would come back with new noses—and the parking lot was full of exotic sports cars. "I

In high school, Meyer saw herself as shy and awkward.

Stephenie and Christiaan "Pancho" Meyer have known each other since childhood.

was practically Cousin Itt in high school. You know, hair in the face, hide from everyone," she told Rose.

During her years in high school, Meyer—due partially to shyness and partially to her Mormon background—dated very little. At church, she had met a young man named Christiaan "Pancho" Meyer but had not spoken more than a few words to him. The two had grown up in the same community but did not spend a great deal of time together until they were teenagers. Neither one could have had a clue that they would end up getting married. "It's funny, because in twenty years of knowing each other, we [had] never had a conversation," Meyer told Megan Irwin at the *Phoenix New Times*. "But we got along so well. On our second official date was when he proposed. He proposed a lot. Over forty times. He would propose every night and I would tell him no every night. It was kind of our end-of-date thing."

When she finally said yes, the two were married during her senior year at Brigham Young University. She graduated in 1997 with a degree in English, then did what many young Mormon wives do—she focused on creating a home for her husband. That is, until an unexpected dream changed everything.

> "He proposed a lot. Over forty times. He would propose every night and I would tell him no every night. It was kind of our end-of-date thing."

Meyer's story of a young girl being tempted by a forbidden fruit—love with an immortal and dangerou vampire—was a familiar one that touched the hearts and emotions of many teen readers.

Developing the Dream

*O*nce Meyer had her dream and began putting thoughts into words, writing became like an obsession for her. Fitting it in with her other responsibilities was not easy, however. "I did a lot of writing at night, because after they [her children] were in bed was the best time to concentrate," she explained to Margolis of *School Library Journal*. "But during the day, I really couldn't stay away from the computer; so I was up and down a lot. I'd sit down and write a few lines, and then I'd get up and give somebody juice, then sit down and write a few lines, and then go change a diaper."

The words came fast and furious. She wrote more than 130,000 words in less than three months. As she put it to Margolis, "It gushed. On a good day, I would write 10 or 12 pages, single-spaced. That's a good chapter and then some. So it was coming very fast. And then there were other parts that were slower, but it pretty much flowed. I began June 2, 2003, and I finished by the end of August."

At first she kept her new passion a secret from everyone. She could just imagine how people would roll their eyes if they heard she was writing a vampire romance. She did not even tell Pancho why she spent so many hours at the computer. "I didn't tell him what I was doing," she admitted in an interview with the Australian *Courier-Mail.* "So he was mystified. And a little irritated that I was hogging the computer all the time. I had as hard a time telling him I was writing a story about vampires as Edward did telling Bella he was one."

Finally, Meyer's sister, Emily Rasmussen, could not stand it any longer. She and Meyer had always been close and talked to each other often. However, for week after week, she did not hear from her sister — what was taking up all of her time and interest? "I called her and said, 'What's going on? Why aren't you calling me anymore?' " said Rasmussen in Irwin's interview. Meyer was hesitant. She hadn't revealed her story to anyone, but this was her sister — from whom she never kept any secrets. "I thought she'd laugh, but it turns out she's a big Buffy [the Vampire Slayer] fan, which I didn't know," recalls Meyer. "She wanted to see it, and, on the one hand, I was very shy about it, but on the other hand, I was in love with it, so I wanted her to see it."

It did not take long to get Emily's response. She adored the story and e-mailed and called her sister, pestering her to send more chapters as fast as possible. Meyer was shocked — and pleased. When she had written this book, she had a very specific audience in mind: herself. "[A] 29-year-old mother of three," she said, laughing, in response to Ed Symkus's questions in the *Morning Sun.* "No one was ever supposed to read this except for me; and if I'd had any idea that anyone else would ever see what I was doing, I would never have been able to finish it because that's way too much pressure."

Emily's enthusiasm did not stop at reading Meyer's story. Next, she encouraged her sister to seek out a publisher for her book. That was a step Meyer had not considered, and when she did, it terrified her. It was time to go back to the computer and do some research.

Although many vampire stories include scenes where crosses and garlic are used to ward off the blood-sucking fiends, Meyer's do not. Her undead characters put a new twist on some of the centuries-old vampire lore.

An Overnight Sensation

Meyer was back on the computer, but this time she was learning instead of writing. She was finding out as much as she could about the publishing process. She knew little to nothing about how to publish a book, and the more research she did about writing query letters and finding agents, the more discouraged she became. It was almost enough to make her quit entirely.

She sent fifteen letters off to agents and then sat back and waited to be rejected. Meyer told the *National Post* that even today, if she is in that section of town, she will drive by the mailbox where she sent the queries out and remember how she felt. It was one of the hardest things she had ever done, because if her book was rejected, it would be painful.

Five of the agents ignored her completely, nine did indeed reject her—and one asked her to send the first three chapters. That agent was Jodi Reamer from Writers House. She agreed to represent Meyer, and after some editing of the manuscript, Reamer sent it off to nine publishers. One of them was Little, Brown and Company. It arrived on the desk of top editor Megan Tingley. She read a draft of the book while she was on

Small World

Editor Megan Tingley '86
and children's literature

Editor Megan Tingley had a strong feeling she was holding a future bestseller when she read Meyer's manuscript. Her hunch was a good one – and she helped create one of Little, Brown and Company's most successful series.

an airplane. Before she landed, she decided to make an offer. "It was the combination of desire and danger that drew me in," she stated in an interview with the *Phoenix New Times.* "I could not put it down and I could not wait for the plane to land so I could sign up the book. On a gut level, I knew I had a bestseller on my hands when I was halfway through the manuscript."

Little, Brown offered $300,000 for a three-book deal. Meyer was thrilled. "I'd been hoping for $10,000 to pay off my minivan," she admitted to *Entertainment Weekly.* She was shocked, however, to discover that her agent had turned down the offer and asked for an unheard of one million dollars. "That was the most surreal day," she recalls in the *Phoenix New Times*. "Eli was with me, so he was thinking Mommy lost her mind for a little while. I was on the phone with Jodi trying to be all professional, 'Yes, I'd love that. That's great,' and then I called my sister and I could hardly talk. Eli was following me around on his play phone going, 'Hahahahaha,' imitating me."

As all the millions of Twilight fans know, the rest is publishing history. *Twilight* was followed by *New Moon, Eclipse,* and *Breaking Dawn.* All of them are huge bestsellers and have been turned into blockbuster movies that have earned millions more than the books. Pancho has been able to retire and return to school, thanks to his wife's success.

A number of bookstores across the country celebrated the release of a new Twilight book by hosting special midnight parties. Employees and customers dressed like their favorite characters, and stores like this one in Montana held special games and events.

Actors Kristen Stewart and Robert Pattinson brought Meyer's characters to life on the big screen. They quickly became some of the most popular actors in the world.

Biss
ZUM MORGENGRAUEN

STEPHENIE MEYE

CARLSEN

◆ THE NO.1 NEW YORK TIMES BEST SELLER ◆

NEW MOON นวจันทรา

STEPHENIE MEYER
นพดล เชฏสวิสต์ แปล

twilight
THE GRAPHIC NOVEL VOLUME 1

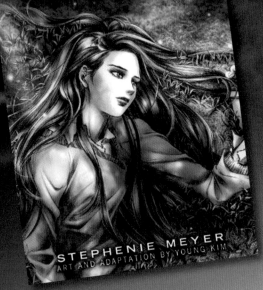

STEPHENIE MEYER
ART AND ADAPTATION BY YOUNG KIM

Meyer's books have been published in many languages and in a variety of formats, including as graphic novels.

Meyer played a large part in the writing and casting of the films. In 2008, approximately 29 million copies of her books were sold. In early 2009, experts estimated that 16 percent of all the books being sold in stores were written by Meyer. That means one in every seven books being purchased was one of hers!

The love story between the human Bella and vampire Edward has captivated readers of all ages throughout the world. It has brought such riches and fame to Meyer that she could never have conceived of—even in her wildest dreams.

What does she have left to do? Plenty!

As the books and movies continued to captivate millions of readers throughout the world, merchandise followed. Stores sold everything from purses and T-shirts to jewelry and hats. Mattel and other companies produced dolls of the main characters, and Twilight products could even be found at perfume and candy counters.

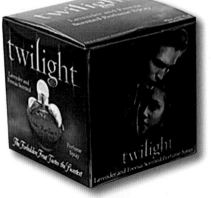

The Breaking Dawn Concert Series, headlined by Justin Furstenfeld of Blue October, celebrated the publication of **Breaking Dawn**. *Between sets, Meyer answered questions from her fans. She revealed that "Hate Me" and other Blue October songs inspired her writing.*

Beyond Vampires and Aliens

E ven though she has written the last book in the Twilight series, Meyer still has many ideas for more ways to keep readers entertained. In the midst of the Twilight frenzy, she published another hugely popular book called *The Host*. Billed as a science-fiction thriller, it was aimed for a somewhat older audience than her previous novels. Like her vampire books, *The Host* soared up the bestseller list and stayed there for weeks. *School Library Journal* reviewed it and stated, "It lives up to the hype, blending science fiction and romance in a way that has never worked so well."

The story was inspired during a routine road trip. While making the long drive down the remote, dull highway from Arizona to Salt Lake City to visit her parents, Meyer needed a way to keep entertained. Slowly, she came up with an idea about an alien that took over a human's body — and then made the mistake of falling in love with a human girl's boyfriend. The girl does everything she can to prevent the growing romance. "I could tell there was something compelling in the idea of such a complicated triangle," Meyer details in an interview with *Readers Read.* "I started writing the outline in a notebook and then fleshed it out as soon as I got to a computer."

It looked as if *The Host* would follow Meyer's other novels and be turned into a film. In autumn 2009, it was announced that a scriptwriter and director had been hired for the project. Once again, Meyer would play a large part in creating the movie. "We wanted Stephenie to be involved in the adaptation and have her endorse and be part of the creative decisions," stated Nick Wechsler, one of the producers, in an interview with MTV. "[Twilight] has proven she knows more about what works than most."

According to Meyer, she has one or two sequels planned for *The Host*. Fans—young and old alike—are eager to read them.

Appearing on television shows like Oprah Winfrey's talk show was a common part of the marketing campaigns for the Twilight books and movies. Everywhere Meyer went, her fans followed!

Meyer is slowly branching out beyond the world of Twilight. On the "Resolution" video set in Malibu, she and Andrew McMahon of Jack's Mannequin talk about their collaboration.

Along with her books, Meyer has been involved in directing a music video with the group Jack's Mannequin, plus she was hired to write *Monster Manual III: Stephenie's Sanctum,* the fourth edition of Wizards of the Coast's popular Dungeon and Dragons game. Why? "The most joyful time writing the Twilight series was when I transformed the vampire and werewolf mythos into something exciting and new. I can't wait to do the same thing with dragons, trolls, and purple worms," she stated in an interview on *BBspot.com.*

It is no surprise that Meyer has chosen to share some of her money, time, and skill with several charities. In the past, she has auctioned off signed manuscripts and advance reading copies to raise money to offset the cost of cancer treatment for a friend. She also agreed to help a skateboard

One of the most fan-friendly celebrities, Meyer stops to have her picture taken with some fans in an airport as she jets from one event to the next.

company market merchandise based on *The Host* in order to raise funds for numerous homeless organizations.

Where will Stephenie Meyer go next? It is hard to say. As a Mormon, wife, and mother of three, she has already achieved things even she could never have predicted. Whether she returns to bloodsucking creatures of the night or soul-stealing aliens — or goes in a different direction altogether — one thing is certain: her fans will follow.

No matter how many books Meyer sells, she will keep working to become a more skillful writer. As she stated to *Entertainment Weekly*, "I want to be a better writer. . . . I read these other authors and I think, 'Now, that's a good writer. I'm never going to reach that level.' But I'm going to be a good storyteller. And what a thing to be!"

CHRONOLOGY

1973	Born in Hartford, Connecticut, on December 24
1977	Family moves to Arizona
1992	Graduates from high school
1996	Marries Christiaan Meyer
1997	Graduates from Brigham Young University
2003	Has the dream that inspired her to write
2005	*Twilight* is published
2006	*New Moon* is published
2007	Short story "Hell on Earth" is published in *Prom Nights from Hell*; *Eclipse* is published
2008	*The Host* and *Breaking Dawn* are published; the movie *Twilight* is released in November
2009	*Monster Manual III: Stephenie's Sanctum* and *The Twilight Saga: The Official Guide* are published; the movie *New Moon* is released in November
2010	*Twilight: The Graphic Novel, Volume 1*, is published; the movie *Eclipse* is released in June

Selected Works

Twilight Series
    Twilight
    New Moon
    Eclipse
    Breaking Dawn
"Hell on Earth" (short story)
The Host
Monster Manual III: Stephenie's Sanctum
The Short Second Life of Bree Tanner
The Twilight Saga: The Official Guide
Twilight: The Graphic Novel, Volume 1

Books

Burton, Ryan, et al. *Female Force Bestsellers: Stephenie Meyer.* Vancouver, WA: Bluewater Productions, 2009.

Gresh, Lois. *The Twilight Companion: The Unauthorized Guide to the Series.* New York: St. Martin's Griffin, 2008.

Shapiro, Marc. *Stephenie Meyer: The Unauthorized Biography of the Creator of the "Twilight" Saga.* New York: Macmillan's Children's Books, 2010.

Works Consulted

Beahm, George. *Bedazzled: A Book about Stephenie Meyer and the Twilight Phenomenon.* Nevada City, California: Underwood Books, 2009.

Briggs, Brian. "Wizards of the Coast Taps Stephenie Meyer to Write *Monster Manual III.*" *BBspot.com,* August 12, 2009. http://www.bbspot.com/News/2009/08/stephenie-meyer-monster-manual.html

Chew, Jeff. "Twilight Author a Part-time Resident of Peninsula on Which Her Books Are Set." *Peninsula Daily News,* September 18, 2009. http://www.peninsuladailynews.com/article/20090918/NEWS/309189992

Cobiella, Kelly. "Stephenie Meyer's Latest Vampire Tale." *CBS Sunday Morning,* August 3, 2008. http://www.cbsnews.com/stories/2008/08/03/sunday/main4317675.shtml

Ditzian, Eric. "Stephenie Meyer's 'The Host' to Become a Movie." *MTV.com,* September 23, 2009. http://www.mtv.com/movies/news/articles/1622110/20090923/story.jhtml

Irwin, Megan. "Charmed." *Phoenix New Times,* July 12, 2007. http://www.phoenixnewtimes.com/2007-07-12/news/charmed/7

Locoge, Benjamin. "Stephenie Meyer: It's Edward Who Forced Me to Write." *Paris Match,* February 22, 2009. http://twilightersanonymous.com/paris-match-new-french-interview-with-twilight-series-author-stephenie-meyer.html

Marglois, Rick. "Love at First Bite." *School Library Journal,* October 1, 2005. http://www.schoollibraryjournal.com/index.asp?layout=talkbackCommentsFull&talk_back_header_id=6260602&articleid=CA6260602

Mills, Tony-Allen. "News Review Interview: Stephenie Meyer." *Times Online,* August 10, 2008. http://entertainment.timesonline.co.uk/tol/arts_and_entertainment/books/article4492238.ece

Rose, Jaimee. "Valley Mom Sinks Her Teeth into Gothic Romance and Finds International Fame." *The Arizona Republic,* November 10, 2007. http://www.azcentral.com/arizonarepublic/arizonaliving/articles/1110stepheniemeyer1110.html?&wired

Smouse, Deb. "Cover Girl Stephenie Meyer: An Interview (Part One)." *All Things Girl,* January–February 2010. http://allthingsgirl.net/everythinggirl/sacrifice-mayjune-2008/cover-girl-stephenie-meyer-an-interview-part-onewith-deb-smouse/

"Stephenie Meyer Reflects on Bright Twilight as DVD Looms." *Courier-Mail*, April 19, 2009. http://www.news.com.au/couriermail/story/0,23739,25346651-5003424,00.html

Symkus, Ed. "Interview with the Vampire Lady: Stephenie Meyer on 'Twilight.' " *MorningSun.net*, November 17, 2008. http://www.morningsun.net/news/entertainment/x1772951064/Interview-with-the-vampire-lady-Stephenie-Meyer-on-Twilight

Unknown. "Interview with Stephenie Meyer." *Readers Read*, June 2008. http://www.readersread.com/features/stepheniemeyer.htm

Valby, Karen. "Stephenie Meyer: Inside the 'Twilight' Saga." *EW.com*, n.d. http://www.ew.com/ew/article/0,,20213067_20213068_20211938,00.html

Wilkinson, Amy. "On the scene: 'Breaking Dawn' Concert Series." *EW.com*, August 2, 2008. http://popwatch.ew.com/2008/08/02/breaking-dawn-c/

On the Internet
The Official Website of Stephenie Meyer
http://www.stepheniemeyer.com/
The Twilight Saga
http://www.thetwilightsaga.com/

PHOTO CREDITS: Cover, p. 1—Steve Granitz/Getty Images; p. 4—Eric Ogden/Corbis; p. 7—Ingo Wagner/dpa/Corbis; p. 8—David Howells/Corbis; pp. 11, 14, 17, 19, 20, 28—Creative Commons 2.0; p. 12—Jordan Strauss/Getty Images; p. 21—Frank Origlia/Getty Images; p. 24—Brad Barket/Getty Images. Every effort has been made to locate all copyright holders of materials used in this book. Any errors or omissions will be corrected in future editions of the book.

INDEX